The Ultimate Coaching Handbook

The skills, techniques and strategies for being a successful and profitable life or business coach

By John Cassidy-Rice & Colette Lees

www.free-nlp.co.uk

Copyright and Legal Information

General Information
Copyright © 2010 by John Cassidy-Rice. All rights reserved.

No part of this publication may be reproduced or transmitted in any form or by any means, mechanical or electronic, including photocopying and recording, or by any information storage and retrieval system, without written permission from the publisher.

Publisher: John Cassidy-Rice, Training Excellence Ltd
www.free-nlp.co.uk

Legal Information
While they have made every effort to verify the information provided in this publication, neither the author nor the publisher assumes any responsibility for errors in, omissions from or different interpretation of the subject matter.

The information herein may be subject to varying laws, regulations and practices in different areas, states and countries. The purchaser or reader assumes all responsibility for use of the information. The publication is not intended as a source of legal or accounting advice and, where appropriate, the advice of a suitably qualified professional should be sought. The author and publisher shall in no event be held liable to any party for any damages arising directly or indirectly from any use of this material. Any perceived slight of specific people or organisations is unintentional.

Every effort has been made to accurately represent this product and its potential and there is no guarantee that you will earn any money using these techniques and ideas. Any links to other websites are for information only and are not warranted for content, performance, accuracy or any other implied or explicit purpose.

About the Author

John Cassidy-Rice

John has been involved in NLP and Personal Development for over 15 years. A recognised and certified International Master NLP Trainer, he has become sought after as a Mentor in NLP. He is the co-founder and principle trainer of NLP Excellence running courses on a national and international basis (www.free-nlp.co.uk)

John has a relaxed, refreshing, humorous and informative style. He is adept at using games, models and music to create an environment where learning is easy and fun. He has a reputation for getting results, a deep understanding of how the mind works and how language affects interaction in life.

His trainings are designed to dramatically increase the creativity, teamwork and performance of organisations and individuals through music and learning technologies. He has worked with many companies such as The Financial Times and Accenture. His work has taken him all over the United Kingdom, and also Internationally in Texas and Florida, USA and Australia.

John is a Managing Partner for the Wizard of Ads, an international marketing company involved in training, research and consultancy in marketing and advertising. John is a dynamic public speaker in this area.

Colette Lees

Colette has an MBA and first class honours degree in Business Studies and has lectured in the Business School at one of the North of England's leading Universities for many years. Her ongoing academic research into Emotional Intelligence underpins her course design & her confident delivery. Prior to her academic career, Colette ran several businesses of her own & is today a director of several private sector companies both in the UK & the US where she acts as a consultant, advisor & coach.

Colette's description of herself as a 'practitioner' of her subject rather than a pure academic allows her to be empathetic with individual real world situations. Her hands on approach and in depth understanding of business structure and relationships allow a unique insight and interventions, which go beyond the limits of traditional training. This together with a relaxed style of delivery enables the subject to be accessible & allows her passion for Emotional Intelligence based coaching to come across in an effective yet approachable manner.

Colette's passion for people and their personal and professional development is the driving force being her career and the subject of a variety of public speaker events.

Contents

Chapter		Page
	Introduction: Becoming the Ultimate Coach	6
1	**What is coaching?**	7
2	**Why have a coach?** • Why the need for coaches is growing • Why individuals and businesses need coaches	9
3	**What coaching involves** • Collaboration between two individuals • Focus on outcomes • Honouring the expertise of the client • Listening more than talking • Giving useful feedback	14

4	**Different types of coaching**
	• Performance coaching
	• Business coaching
	• Executive coaching
	• Internal coaching
	• Management coaching
	• Life coaching
	• What coaching is not
	   o Training
	   o Consulting
	   o Therapy or counselling
	   o Mentoring
		16

5	**What makes a good coach?**	22

	1. Confidence 2. Awareness 3. Clarity 4. Curiosity 5. Patience 6. Empathy 7. Integrity 8. Challenge 9. Creativity 10. Compassion 11. Detachment 12. Personality	
6	**The COACH model** • Clarity • Options • Action • Character • Help and support	26
7	**The keys to coaching** 1. Reaching for the moon and other achievable goals 2. When the most important points are left unsaid 3. Why questions are the answer 4. Putting the power of many brains to work 5. How to get action when nothing else works 6. How to clear immovable obstacles on the road to success 7. Making feedback the key to getting results	29

| 8 | **The process of coaching** | 87 |
| 9 | **Developing a coaching mission statement** | 89 |

Introduction: Becoming the Ultimate Coach

The huge growth in coaching in recent years has led to many more people being aware of how having a coach can improve their lives.

However, the truth is that many people have set themselves up as coaches with little understanding of the skills, techniques and strategies that help clients achieve their maximum potential.

Equally, many have failed to take the necessary steps to make sure they have a sound proposition in place that helps them make money if they work on their own or that gives full value to the organisation when they work in business.

This guide sets out step-by-step the key skills, techniques and strategies that will help you be a coach that gets great results for your clients.

> *"You'll be able to make a huge difference to the lives of others."*

It also shows you the key issues you need to consider if you are to have commercial success as well.

When you know how to use this knowledge to the full, you'll be able to make a huge difference to the lives of others while achieving rewards and success in your own career.

When you've read this book, you'll be well positioned to be a great coach.

To your success
John Cassidy-Rice & Colette Lees

1. What is Coaching?

The term 'coaching' is so widely used in many different contexts that it's worth getting clear about what coaching is and what it is not.

The typical dictionary definitions don't help as they usually refer to training sports teams and athletes or else they talk about methods of transport.

Naturally many people are familiar with what coaches can do in sport and this can be both useful and unhelpful for those who coach in other areas.

> *"The typical idea of a coach is someone sitting on the sidelines shouting to run faster or try harder."*

Everybody knows that sports stars like Tiger Woods or Roger Federer have a coach and it's widely felt that the quality of the team coach is key to the success of a football or rugby team.

But sport can give people the wrong idea of what a coach does. The typical idea of a sports coach is probably someone sitting on the sidelines shouting to run faster or try harder. And that's not a concept most people can easily place in other areas of their lives.

The lack of clarity and awareness around what coaching is shows how much the field has grown in recent years and why there is great potential for it to become even more important in future.

There has been some evidence of people performing a coaching role within businesses for around 50 years but it's only in the last 20 – 30 years that the discipline has become more mainstream and organised.

The field of 'life coaching' for example is even more recent. We'll look more closely at the different types of coaching in chapter 3.

To get back to what coaching is, here's how Wikipedia defines it:

> *"Coaching is a method of directing, instructing and training a person or group of people, with the aim to achieve some goal or develop specific skills."*

This is a useful way to describe coaching but it doesn't go deeply enough into what is actually happening in a coaching relationship.

In his book 'Awaken the Giant Within', the personal development guru Tony Robbins – described as the father of life coaching – explains coaching as follows:

> *"A coach is committed to helping you be the best you can be. A coach will challenge you not let you off the hook.*
>
> *Sometimes coaches can teach you new information, new strategies and skills... Sometimes a coach doesn't even teach you something new but they remind you of what you need to do at just the right moment and push you to do it."*

That paints a picture of coaching which is about someone using a specific set of skills, strategies and techniques to help others achieve their full potential by taking action, overcoming blocks and improving their expertise.

But surely we're capable of doing that on our own? Why would someone need a coach?

Why Have A Coach?

As businesses and individuals have survived and prospered for many years you might wonder why we have a growing need for coaches.

Let's look first at why the need for coaching is becoming greater and then look at some of the specific ways in which coaches can help people.

Why the need for coaches is growing
Here are some reasons why the demand for coaches is on the increase.

- **More flexible careers**

    These days the idea of people building a career for life within the same organisation is no longer as common as it used it be.

    This has implications both for businesses and for the people who work in them.

    Individuals have to learn to manage their own careers and make decisions such as whether to move jobs and how to develop their skills.

    Organisations have to be able to attract talent and need to be able to get results from them in a much shorter timeframe than before.

    > *"The pace of change is faster that ever and people need to know how to react quickly."*

    They have to use different techniques to manage people because they can no longer rely on the old approaches to people management.

In these circumstances, businesses have to put more effort into creating collaboration and teamwork.

- **Greater pace of change**
From technology to politics and the environment, things are changing at a much faster pace and people need to be able to react quickly to these changes.

Many people don't have the breadth of experience they need to be able to handle these changes and that's why they often want to turn to an external adviser.

There is also a growing gap between what people learned in the early stages of their career and what they need to do to prosper in the new environment.

- **More entrepreneurs**
A combination of economic circumstances and the changing face of organisations mean many people who would previously have stayed in large organisations as now setting up their own businesses.

Often these are people with many talents and ideas but typically they have not learned the skills necessary to succeed as an entrepreneur.

They often see an advantage in having expert help to guide them through the process.

- **Complicated lives**
In the same way that the face of business has changed, people's personal lives are typically more complicated than before.

People who previously would have relied on a family network may be living away from their natural support base and could be juggling their own family responsibilities with a career.

The pace of technology means most people are living their lives with a constant supply of information and are often unable to stand back and see what is most important.

- **More skilled coaches**
  As the demand for coaches has grown, the field has become more organised and the quality of coaches in most fields has improved significantly.

  > *"Coaches are getting better and the results they achieve for their clients are being more widely noticed."*

  As a result, the coaches are getting better and the results they achieve for their clients are being more widely noticed.

  As people notice others' lives being improved by working with coaches, they see the value of having a coach in their own lives.

Why individuals and businesses need coaches

There are many specific reasons why an individual or a business may use a coach.

Sometimes it's to meet a specific need – e.g. when someone changes their role in an organisation or there is a major culture change – and sometimes it's to improve performance over the longer term.

We'll look at some specific examples in case studies throughout this book but here are some of the general benefits individuals and businesses get from working with a coach:

- **Accountability:** The pressures of immediate daily deadlines often stop people taking the action they need to on immediate issues. A coach can help you stay focused on the bigger picture.

- **Clarity:** A coach can help you focus on the bigger picture, get clear on where you are going rather than getting bogged down on day to day issues.

> "A coach can help you stay focused on the bigger picture."

- **Confidence:** Having to explain and discuss an issue with a coach first helps you develop belief in it before taking it to a wider audience.

- **Team building:** Coaches can work both with teams and with individuals to improve overall performance.

- **Sounding board:** Especially at senior levels, it's often difficult to have someone within the organisation you can talk to about your ideas before they're fully developed. A coach can fulfil that role.

- **Contacts and resources:** A good coach with the right experience can suggest other people you can contact to make further progress and will know other resources you can use to get faster results.

- **Specific expertise:** Sometimes it's appropriate to have a coach who has specific experience you can draw on directly e.g. experience of a particular country or market.

- **Motivation:** For people who work on their own, a coach can provide the regular contact to keep you motivated. For those who work in businesses, a coach has the benefit of being outside the regular politics that can get you down.

- **Culture change:** A coach can help an individual change the way they work and can have the same effect on an organisation when they work with a whole team.

- **Challenge:** Sometimes your friends and colleagues don't ask the difficult questions because they don't want to upset you or they are too busy with their own issues. A good coach will always make you stop and think.

These are just some of the benefits that individuals get from working with coaches.

We'll see many more as we look at case studies and examples in the rest of this book.

2. What Coaching Involves

As we saw in chapter 1, it's still hard to find a clear definition of coaching.

This means there are many different interpretations of what it is. So in this chapter, we'll look at what coaching involves.

In the following chapter, we consider the different types of coaching and also clarify what coaching is not.

- **Collaboration between two individuals**
  A coaching relationship is normally a confidential arrangement between two individuals.

  Even if a company were paying, the discussions between the coach and the client would not be reported back to the company.

  Therefore the key to the success of the relationship will be the degree of trust and confidence between the coach and the client.

- **Focus on outcomes**
  The coach's priority is usually to help the client define specific outcomes and take action to get them.

  The coach's job is to help the client get results and not just get a vague sense of feeling better.

- **Honouring the expertise of the client**
  The coach is not there to tell the client what to do. Their job is to help the client decide what action to take to get results.

The coach may or not be an expert in the client's subject matter. This usually doesn't matter. Their job is to help the client decide what to do and then use their own skills to get the results.

- **Listening more than talking**

    The coach is there to help the individual work it out for themselves rather than to give them specific solutions. So the key is to let the client do the talking.

    > "The coach is not there to tell the client what to do."

    In business most people are in a rush and few people can find someone to listen to them. Sometimes just having a sympathetic ear can make issues seem less important as well as giving you space to work out solutions.

- **Giving useful feedback**

    The role of the coach is not to pass judgment but to help people draw their own conclusions.

    A good coach will therefore not say: 'You didn't make a very good job of that'.

    They are more likely to ask the clients to reflect on the situation themselves and see what they learned from it.

    That can mean drawing their attention to things they have not noticed but doing so in a very diplomatic way.

3. Different Types of Coaching

Coaching splits into many different categories, including:

- **Performance coaching**
  The best known type of coaching is performance coaching and this is often applied to specific areas of expertise such as sports or music.

  Here the coach's job is to help the client get the best results possible in their field of talent or expertise.

  Even in sports this is not simply a matter of skill. It is often largely an element of psychology.

  As a result, there are many opportunities for performance coaches even in fields where they don't have the top skills themselves.

  The people who made the best sports coaches, for example, were often not those who won most medals.

  In business, performance coaches can work with clients in specific fields such as public speaking, media interviews or recruitment.

- **Business coaching**
  In business coaching, the coach works with an individual to achieve specific results relating to their business.

  It may involve working to achieve a specific objective – such as profit improvement - or deal with a one-off situation – such as a new role – or it may be an ongoing relationship.

Business coaches can work with people in organisations or with self-employed people and entrepreneurs.

Business coaching can involve working with individuals or groups.

- **Executive coaching**
Executive coaching is a sub-set of business coaching where the coach works with a director or senior executive in an organisation.

Often executive coaches are themselves experienced executives but this does not always have to be the case.

- **Internal coaching**
Many larger organisations have people designated as coaching specialists to work with other colleagues. They may be full-time specialist coaches or they may be other managers who are trained to work as coaches with people who are not in their own management line.

There are some advantages in having internal coaches over employing an external coach. The most obvious advantage is that it is often cheaper for the organisation than employing an external coach. This means the benefit can be extended to a wider range of people.

Another advantage is that internal coaches are often more familiar with specific issues that apply to the organisation. This gives them the prospect of greater empathy with the client and also the possibility of doing something about it.

One of the downsides of internal coaches is that they do not offer the outside perspective that an external coach can bring. Also clients may be less open with internal coaches even though they would be assured of complete confidentiality.

- **Management coaching**
  Coaching is a skill as well as a label and often the best person to coach an individual in a business setting is their own line manager.

The challenge is for both client and manager to put their management relationship to one side and for the manager to get into the habit of asking questions to help develop the person, rather than telling them what to do.

This approach can be very powerful but can be a challenge depending on the individuals involved and the culture of the organisation.

- **Life coaching**
  Life coaching is a growing field where the coach works with the client in a much more rounded way in all areas of their lives.

The relationship between a life coach and their client is more likely to be a personal one rather than one driven by the client's business.

Career issues however are likely to be an important part of the coach's work with the client.

From the coach's viewpoint, a downside of life coaching is that the typical fees are often lower than for business coaching.

What coaching is not

So we've looked at some definitions that cover what coaching involves.

There are a number of other fields where specialists work with clients to help overcome problems and get better results. Although there are often overlaps between the fields, it is useful to be aware of the differences.

- **Training**

    Training is where an individual or group learns how to do a specific skill.

    With training, you would expect to undertake a program and come out of it with specific knowledge enabling you to undertake a specific task.

    For example, you could go on a training course to learn the specific skills required to become good at public speaking.

    A coach however, would work with you on an ongoing basis to make the most of these skills and overcome any obstacles to success.

    Working with the coach, you may develop a programme for speaking at certain events and you'd discuss with your coach how to make the most of the opportunities.

- **Consulting**

    In a consulting assignment, a problem may be handed over to external experts for them to analyse the situation and make recommendations.

    While the consultants may speak to people in the company for their views, the job of the consultants is to use their expertise to suggest a way forward.

A coach on the other hand may work with a group of people from the company and facilitate them to come up with solutions.

The distinction is that the consultants are recommending a course of action to the company or individual, while the coach is helping them work out their own best outcome using their own experience and knowledge.

- **Therapy or counselling**
  Therapy or counselling is where someone addresses a particular problem that may be holding them back.

  Therapeutic work tends to be looking at problems that have arisen in the past and helping people to go back and resolve these. This work usually involves more specialist psychiatric or psychological expertise.

  > *"Therapy usually addresses feelings and emotions, while coaching is more outcome-driven."*

If an executive has serious problems about nerves when in speaking public, for example, they may begin by attending training or working with their coach.

If the problem persists and is more deep-rooted, some sort of therapy may be suggested to resolve these problems from the past.

Therapy usually addresses feelings and emotions, while coaching is usually more results and outcome driven, while giving proper attention to the person's feelings.

In that sense, therapy is more about fixing the past while coaching is about influencing the future.

- **Mentoring**

    A mentor is typically someone with very specific experience relevant to the client – for example someone who has run a company giving advice to a new managing director.

    They will usually give guidance and advice based on their own experiences in similar circumstances.

    Mentoring arrangements are often informal and are very common for people in new situations.

    Although individual arrangements may vary, a mentor may make specific suggestions to a client based on their own experience.

    In the same situation, a coach would help the clients to work out their own solution.

    So a mentor would be more inclined to suggest specific solutions, while a coach would guide you to develop your own.

4. What Makes A Good Coach?

Now that we've looked at what coaching involves, let's cover what makes a good coach.

Below we've listed 12 characteristics of a good coach. Following this section, we've included an analysis tool to help you evaluate how you measure up and identify where you can improve your skills.

1. **Confidence**
    Nobody wants a coach to be hesitant and uncertain, clients look to a coach to create a clear sense of direction.

2. **Awareness**
    A good coach is both self-aware – in that they know their own strengths and their own mood in the moment – and they are aware of their surroundings.

    They take into account what is happening with the client and in the surrounding environment.

3. **Clarity**
    The coach's job is to help the client see the real problem and to identify exactly what needs to be done. The coach therefore cannot be confused and uncertain.

4. **Curiosity**
    Coaches have to be interested in other people. As the key to good coaching is often asking the right question, the coach has to be taking enough interest in the client to come up with the question.

5. **Patience**

    Although your job as a coach is to move people forward as fast as possible, you must give them time to progress at their own pace.

    Don't be tempted to jump in too quickly with your own ideas and suggestions.

6. **Empathy**

    Try to put yourself in their situation and let them see that you understand what they are facing. Empathy doesn't mean buying in to their problems or excuses.

7. **Integrity**

    The key to any coaching relationship is earning the client's trust and keeping it.

    > *"The key to any coaching relationship is earning the client's trust and keeping it."*

    What happens in a coaching relationship must be between you and the client only.

    Equally you must never discuss other clients with them.

8. **Challenge**

    Your job as a coach is to get people out of their comfort zones so you need to find the right way and best time to push them to new levels of achievement.

9. **Creativity**

    You need to help the client find new ways of looking at things. Sometimes that will come from asking the right questions, sometimes it will be from stories you tell. Often it will come from suggesting a different approach. Judgemental.

10. **Compassion**

    Compassion is about respecting the client for who they are and being non-judgmental. Your job is to help them move forward not make judgement on how they got here.

11. **Detachment**

    You stay focused on the objectives without getting caught up in the details. You don't get personally involved in their issues.

12. **Personality**

    Without losing that sense of detachment, you should be yourself in the relationship with your client.

> *"Your job is to help them move forward not make judgement on how they got here."*

They will feel more relaxed and ready to open themselves to you if you are natural and act as yourself.

Evaluating Your Coaching Skills

Use the following chart to rate where you are for each of these 12 key coaching skills. Rate yourself 10 when you believe your skills in an area are excellent and 1 when you feel they are poor.

	1	2	3	4	5	6	7	8	9	10
Confidence										
Awareness										
Clarity										
Curiosity										
Patience										
Empathy										
Integrity										
Challenge										
Creativity										
Detachment										
Compassion										
Personality										

Identify the 3 skills where you had the lowest scores and decide how you can improve on each score.

1. _____

2. _____

3. _____

6. The COACH Model

Successful coaching is not just sitting down with a client for a nice chat.

To make the most of a coaching relationship, it's useful to follow a structured approach.

There are a number of structured approaches or models to coaching that are useful and one of the best is known as the COACH model.

Here are the keys to using this model.

Clarity

Often the first part of a coaching task is to get clarity – both on where the person wants to go and where they are now.

The key to this is asking the right questions. You want to start by getting a picture of where they want to go – perhaps in relation to the coaching session itself or in their life as a whole.

So initial questions could include:
- What are you looking to achieve?
- What is your long-term goal?
- What do you want to get out of this session?

Part of clarity is also finding out why they are where they are:
- Tell me more about your current situation
- What have you done so far to change?
- What's stopping you from getting what you want?
- Why haven't you achieved more?

So the key to clarity is understanding what they want to achieve, where they are now and what steps they have already taken.

Options

Once you have clarity, you can help them begin to develop options for moving forward.

Initially the aim is to develop as many options as possible – not to make judgments about which might be the right ones.

> *"Once you have clarity, you can help them develop options for moving forward."*

When a wide range of options have been identified, the role of the coach is to ask questions, help the client narrow them down and find the best way forward. Typical questions include:

- What would you do if there were no limits?
- What would be the advantages of that?
- What are the drawbacks of that?
- Which one would you choose if it was only up to you?
- What would be the best choice?
- Which options inspire you?
- What's stopping you from doing that?

Action

When you work through all the options and make a decision, a course of action is chosen.

The client has to identify specific action steps to make this happen. These should be specific steps that will move them towards the goals they have clearly identified.

The action steps need to be things they can control. The steps can be large or small, depending on the client and the circumstances, but they should be stretching and challenging overall.

The client must set all the action steps and they should set the timetable. Your job is to help them by challenging them and filling in the detail.

Character

Next you need to work with them to identify what they need to change about their character to get the results they are looking for.

- Are they prepared to take the first step?
- What inner resources do they need to develop?
- Are they up for it?
- Will they step outside their comfort zone?

Help and Support

Finally as a coach, you need to help them identify what support they need from others to get what they want.

- Do they need buy-in from bosses or colleagues?
- Do they need support from friends and family?
- If they don't get it, will it affect their ability to get the goal?

This gives us an overall model to work with. Our next task is to develop the specific skills to put this into action.

7.1 Keys to Coaching:
Reaching for the Moon and Other Achievable Goals

On May 25th 1961, John F Kennedy spoke to a joint session of the US Congress and made a comment that many thought was crazy.

This was a man recently embarrassed by the failed attempt to overthrow the Cuban government and what he said that day took the world by surprise.

> *"I believe that this nation should commit itself to achieving the goal, before this decade is out, of landing a man on the moon and returning him safely to the earth."*

What he was doing was setting a challenge for his people. Giving them a vision they could look towards and believe in.

As he said himself, he was setting a goal.

There is much we can learn from these few words about how setting clear goals can inspire people towards greater results.

Why set goals?
Everybody seems to talk about goal setting but is it really that useful? Here are some of the reasons why goal setting can make a big difference in your life.

- **Clear sense of direction**
  In any journey, you need a clear sense of the precise destination you are aiming for. Without that, it's easy to drift and it becomes hard to make decisions.

- **Allows measurement**

    When you know your target, you can measure your progress towards achieving it. That allows you to decide whether you need to make changes in what you are doing to get to your desired outcome.

- **Provides motivation**

    Having something specific to aim for helps you develop the drive to achieve it – especially when you have made the goal compelling and precise.

    Being able to see the progress you are making also gives you encouragement to make further progress.

    > *"Having something specific to aim for helps you develop the drive to achieve it."*

- **Makes a commitment**

    Although it's not necessary to share your goals with others, doing so can help encourage you to succeed.

    Kennedy's public commitment to reaching the moon means he was not only committed to making it happen, the whole country would have felt a sense of pride in making it happen.

- **Help you develop action steps**

    When you have a clear final destination in mind, you can work out exactly what you need to do to get you there.

    First you can establish distinct milestones on the road to where you want to be, then you can work out the action steps needed to reach each milestone.

- **Make decisions clearer and establish priorities**
  Clear goals make it easier to make choices. You can decide a course of action depending on whether it takes you closer towards or further away from your goals. You can decide the degree of importance to attach to something based on how much closer it will get you to your goal.

So if goal setting is that great, why do so many people not bother? Surely many of them go on to become successful?

Well certainly many people have become successful without setting clear goals. But how much more successful could they have been if they had taken time to establish a clear direction.

> "People who take time to set clear goals end up more successful than those who do not."

Many studies have shown that people who take time to set clear goals and do it properly end up more successful than those who do not.

The truth is many people talk about goal setting but few get round to doing it properly. As a coach, you can make a big difference to someone's life if you help them set clear goals and objectives.

There are many reasons why people fail to set goals properly.

- **They don't see why it's important**
  Of course people need a reason to do something that might involve a bit of work.

  That's why as a coach, you need to show people the real benefits of setting goals and the way it can improve results and make life better.

- **They've 'tried it before'**
  Many people have had the experience of setting goals and then getting disillusioned when things didn't work out. There can be many reasons why this happened ranging from not setting good goals to finding they lose interest after a while.

  A coach helps people set good goals and stay on track.

- **They're 'too busy'**
  When you have lots to do today, the idea of sitting down and imagining what life might be like at some stage in the future can seem self-indulgent.

  A coach can show clients how setting goals is a valuable investment of time that actually helps you feel better organised and less stressed.

  > "A coach helps people set good goals and stay on track."

- **They can't do it alone**
  Often trying to write your own goals seems pointless. Some people find it easy to dream up goals that are either unattainable or are so easy they are pointless.

  A good coach will help people develop goals that are attainable but stretching.

Areas of life for goal setting

Individuals can set goals in any area of life, including:
- Business or career
- Love and romance

- Health and fitness
- Friends and social life
- Money and finances
- Creativity
- Spirituality

The keys to successful goal setting
It's clear that some goals work and others don't so let's take a look at the characteristics of a successful goal.

- **The ingredients of a good goal**
    There are certain characteristics of goals that will work well. One of the most useful ways of summarizing these characteristics is through the letters ACHIEVE. The keys to this are as follows:

    o **As If Now:** A good goal is stated **'as if now'** meaning in the present tense. For example, it is 31st December and I have achieved…

    A goal stated in the future will easily sound like a dream.

    o **Clear and Specific:** There's no point in setting a goal to be rich for example. You have to say exactly what you mean – specify how much money.

    If Kennedy had set a goal of simply travelling in space, for example, it would have made much less impact.

    Note how he also is specific about 'returning him safely to earth.' Many people set goals that look fine in isolation but don't cover all the possibilities.

- **Hittable:** Your goal must be physically possible even if it is stretching.

Though Kennedy's goal seemed far-fetched, the Soviets already had a man in space so it was possible to imagine it happening.

Note that many people would have said it was impossible. There will always be people who question whether a good goal can be reached.

As well as being possible, it has to be realistic in the context of the individual.

If one person can be a millionaire, then it seems logical that many others can be as well. But it's not

> *"Goals have often been described as dreams with deadlines."*

a realistic option for the individual who is not prepared to work hard or take some risk.

Kennedy's goal was realistic as the US already had a space program. The same goal from the leader of a small country or one with limited capability to launch space missions would have been unrealistic even if it were technically achievable.

The coach's job is to stretch the client while keeping them rooted in reality. Without a coach, people often make mistakes on judging what is reasonable – either setting their standards too low or too high.

- **In a Positive Direction:** You should set goals for what you want to achieve rather than what you want to get away from. For example, you'd set a goal to have more money rather than to pay off debt.

- **Exciting:** The goal must involve an element of challenge in order to keep you motivated – even if the challenge doesn't quite involve going to the moon.

  The goal also has to be something you personally want. A goal for someone else is not going to deliver the same results.

  With Kennedy's goal, everybody in the US was involved in the dream he was sharing.

- **Verifiable:** You must be able to know that you have achieved your goal. This applies both to the 'what' and the 'when'.

  So the outcome must be measurable.

  You need to have your personal equivalent of Neil Armstrong's walk on the moon to give you a moment to celebrate.

  And without a clear timetable for achievement, a goal is nothing but a dream.

  In fact, goals have often been described as dreams with deadlines.

The timetable not only gives you a definite point by which you will achieve the goal, it will also help you measure progress at specific points on the way.

Kennedy's goal was a good one because he attached a clear timescale to it when he said 'by the end of this decade'.

A goal left without a deadline can be easily forgotten or excuses can be made that it will happen 'soon'.

- **Ecological:** Your goal should be something that does not harm others and does not stop you doing other things that are important.

For example, when you set goals in your business life, you need to make sure they do not stop you taking care of your health or building your personal relationships.

Action point

Here are some examples of goals that people often set. Notice how you can improve each of them by following the ACHIEVE approach. We've completed the first example.

Original goal	ACHIEVE goal
I want to make a lot of money	*I have earned £200,000 in my business during 2009*
We want to make more sales	
I want to have a better relationship	
I want more customers	
I need to lose weight	

So that covers the process of setting a good goal. Let's have a look now at some of the ways in which we can improve our goals to make them more effective.

- **How to make the outcomes compelling**

    Following the ACHIEVE process helps to create a goal that people will be ready to move towards. But there are steps you can follow to make it even more compelling.

    One way to do that is to make sure that it is as specific as possible and have the client use all their senses in creating it.

    You can do that by having them draw a picture of it or using a photograph to represent it. The more specific the better.

    Don't have them set a goal of having a new car. Make them specify all the details – make, colour, model, engine size, fittings.

    Have them imagine what it will be like to have achieved the goal and then emphasise all the senses in their imagination – see it in bright colours, hear all the sounds, make the feeling real.

    All of these steps will help the goal become ingrained in the unconscious mind and make it easier for them to use all of their resources to achieve the goal.

- **Distinguishing between needs and wants**

    Compelling goals are based on what people want to do rather than what they need to do.

    Where someone expresses a goal as being something they need to do, help them find a way to really **want** it.

Get them to list out the reasons their life will be better when they have achieved it.

Even a goal of making money can come across as something they need to do – for example to repay debt - and this will make it more difficult to achieve.

So find a way to make it appealing so that they will be motivated towards it.

- **Separating the 'shoulds' from the 'musts'**
We all have things we know we should do – lose weight, spend more time with family, reduce time wasting on the internet.

> *"Where someone expresses a goal as being something they need to do, help them find a way to really want it."*

But 'should' goals are never compelling. We start out with good intentions and lose interest after a while.

As a coach, you need to help clients distinguish between 'should' and 'must' so that they devote maximum energy to things they know they must do.

- **Recognising the difference between performance goals and outcome goals**
There is a difference between goals that are set based on performance and those that reflect outcomes.

A performance goal might, for example, be 'make 25% more profit on every sale'

An outcome goal would be 'increase profits by 25% this year'

There is a role for both types of goal but outcome goals are generally more compelling. Performance goals can be useful as steps towards achieving outcome goals.

Setting the client up for success

That's all about the process of goal setting but setting goals is only the starting point. In a sense, setting the goals is the easy bit.

The real challenge is about staying on course to achieve them.

We'll cover some of the elements of that in the later Keys, but there are a few things you as the coach can do during the goal setting process to set them up for a greater chance of success later.

- **Turn dreams into realities with an action plan**
  If you follow the ACHIEVE process, the client will have a great goal to move towards.

- However, they are only going to achieve that goal if you help them develop a plan for turning it into action.

  One way to approach this is to imagine you have already achieved the goal and then work backwards noting all the steps that you completed – and when – in order to get there.

  One advantage of this approach is that it requires the client to go into the future and imagine what it will be like actually having achieved the goal. This helps inspire them to action.

  Alternatively, you can just work out exactly what you need to do step by step to get to the desired destination.

This could result in development of a number of milestones and sub-goals on the way.

So, if the goal for example, is to double profits in the next year – the sub-goals or milestones might include:
- Winning five new clients
- Recruiting two new salespeople
- Launching three new products
- Reducing costs per sale by 25%

These should ideally have specific timescales attached.

Another key to moving clients towards their goal is having them identify one action they can take in the next 24 hours to move them towards their goal.

This builds in the habit of taking action.

- **Identifying what resources and help you need**
Part of the process of turning goals into an action plan is identifying what resources and help they need to achieve the goal.

> *"The process of achieving a goal can grind to a halt if another person blocks progress."*

This may be a simple step of listing what you'll need to move to the next step. But it could be a complex process of identifying exactly what you'd need and looking at potential obstacles.

Often the process of achieving a goal can grind to a halt because another person blocks progress or the necessary resources aren't available.

Identify these contingencies as early as possible and where necessary, work out strategies for what you will do if they don't work out in your favour.

- **Make it easy to stay on course**
   In a later Key, we'll talk in more detail about the process of motivation and about how to overcome disappointment if it occurs.

- You can take action now to avoid disappointment later by ensuring that the goals follow the ACHIEVE process. It's useful in setting goals to talk about what would be acceptable and what would be disappointing.

   Achieving 90% of a challenging goal may be more satisfying than reaching an easier goal.

Case study: Jane the designer

Jane had been running a design agency for three years and was doing well financially but was stressed out working long hours.

She turned to a business coach to help organise her life better and maintain financial success combined with a better quality of life.

Though the issue affected all areas of her life, her coach suggested that working on the business would improve things in all the other areas.

After they discussed her situation, Jane realised she'd been so busy setting up the business and looking after clients that she'd never stopped to establish what was important to her.

Working with her coach, they established clear goals for what she was looking to achieve. She set goals for several areas, including:
- Developing business with existing clients
- How many hours to work ever day
- Profits she wanted

She quickly found she was wasting time chasing every project and started focusing on developing existing projects. By paying attention to the number of hours in the office, she cut out distractions and delegated more. Her profits increased when she cut costs to achieve her targets.

Jane found that sitting down and setting some goals made her priorities a lot clearer and helped her focus on what's important.

She has since set goals in many other areas of her life with great results.

Action step

- Decide an area of your life to set a goal

- Create a single goal in this area using the ACHIEVE formula and other tips

- Create specific action steps to turn this goal into reality, identifying what resources and help you need

Summary and Conclusions

Why set goals?
- Clear sense of direction
- Allows measurement
- Provides motivation
- Makes a commitment
- Help you develop action steps
- Make decisions clearer and establish priorities

Goals can be in any key area of your life
- Business or career
- Love and romance
- Health and fitness
- Friends and social life
- Money and finances
- Creativity
- Spirituality

The keys to setting good goals
- ACHIEVE the goal
    - As If Now
    - Clear and Specific
    - Hittable
    - In a Positive Direction
    - Exciting
    - Verifiable
    - Ecological
- Make the outcomes compelling
- Find a way to turn 'needs' into 'wants'
- Drop the 'shoulds' and focus on the 'musts'

- Use outcome goals rather than performance goals

Set the client up for success
- Turn dreams into realities by creating an action plan
- Identify what resources and help you need
- Make it easy to stay on course

In conclusion

On September 16th 1969, when the astronauts Neil Armstrong, Buzz Aldrin and Michael Collins stood before another joint session of Congress, they had returned from their successful moon landing the previous May achieving the goal set by Kennedy eight years earlier.

Kennedy's vision received a mixed reception at the time – many claimed it was ridiculous and impossible. It was certainly challenging but it was also clear, specific and motivating.

Circumstances meant he was not the person to make it happen. But the way he expressed the goal undoubtedly inspired those who did.

7.2 Keys to Coaching:
When the Most Important Points Are Left Unsaid

When AGD Enterprises took over its biggest competitor, its owners were sure it was guaranteed enormous success.

After all, they'd spent a great deal of time in conversations with the company's senior management and they'd carefully looked over all the financial data.

So they were unpleasantly surprised when they discovered that things were not going as well as they'd expected.

Sales began to slow and some of the best people were leaving at a much faster rate than expected.

They began to wonder if they'd missed something important during the conversations they had as part of the evaluation process before they made the purchase.

Why is it important to listen at 100%?
In any conversation, the importance of listening to what the other person is saying may seem obvious.

But the ability to listen very closely is a very rare skill that can make a significant difference to your success as a coach.

The truth is that most of us only give part of out attention when the other person is talking.

Part of our mind is on something else. Often we are thinking more about what we are going to say next rather than listening to what the speaker is saying. This is known as inactive listening.

Active listening is giving 100% attention to the other person. Here are some reasons why developing the skill of active listening is important.

- How people speak is almost as important as what they say – the words they choose and their tone of voice tell a big story

- You can learn a lot from what people don't say – what they want to avoid talking about

- Observing body language can reveal a lot about what is really going on in someone's mind

- Through active listening, you can note how the other person speaks and also watch their body language so that you can adapt your own to make them feel more comfortable and build rapport

- Demonstrating that you are listening actively will make the client feel more relaxed and willing to open up with you

What is active listening?
With active listening, we are giving our full attention to the other person.

That means leaving all our other concerns to one side during the conversation.

It means paying full attention to the other person with all our senses. Observing – listening with our eyes – is as important in evaluating what the other person is saying as hearing what they say.

We use what we pick up and feed it back into the conversation to help it develop. This not only makes the other person feel that you are paying attention to them it helps develop the conversation in areas that would not be possible listening only to the words.

How to listen actively
There are several techniques you can use to become an active listener. Here are some key points.

> *"Listening with our eyes is as important as hearing what the other person is saying."*

- **Prepare beforehand**
  Get ready for conversation in advance by reviewing any relevant notes and thinking about what might come up

- **Set aside personal issues**
  Make sure you leave all your other concerns and issues to one side during the conversation

- **Acknowledge your emotions**
  Put your own emotions aside – if you are stressed or have a major issue on your mind – or reschedule the conversation for a time when you are able to devote your full attention to it

- **Exclude disruptions**
  Close the door, switch off your phone, put away any other documents

- **Forget your own opinions**
  Put aside your own views about the matter being discussed. Focus entirely on what the person is saying

- **Set up the right environment**

  Where possible set up the environment of the discussion so that you can both be comfortable and get a clear view of each other

- **Use non-visual cues**

  Show you are listening for example by nodding your head, saying a few words or smiling as appropriate. In doing this, don't agree or disagree with them but encourage them to keep talking

- **Be involved**

  Actively respond where necessary by asking questions to encourage them to talk more or by answering their questions

- **Check your understanding**

  Make sure you have understood correctly by restating what they have said and asking, "So you're saying…"

- **Summarise**

  Repeat what they have said and check you have interpreted it correctly and give them a chance to clarify or add more

Case study: Simon the manager

Simon had recently been promoted to head a customer service team that had been facing a number of client complaints and was given the task of sorting it out.

He held several meetings with his team to find out what issues were causing problems but he found he was making little progress as they would only make general comments or say everything was fine.

Getting frustrated at the lack of progress, he learned some of the secrets of active listening and sat down individually with a few members of the team.

Gradually he was able to piece together a story and identified issues about the way the group had previously been managed.

> *"Showing he was genuinely listening to their concerns had helped develop an atmosphere of trust."*

People had been told to follow processes exactly and alternative views were not tolerated.

After a few sessions, he was able to make some progress in encouraging people to share their concerns and ideas on an individual basis. This led on to some issues coming out into the open and the team coming together to address them.

He realised that the process of showing he was genuinely listening to their concerns had helped develop an atmosphere of trust and that this had led to positive change.

Action step

- List 7 barriers that discourage active listening

- Think of the next time you will be in a conversation where it's important to give the other person 100% attention. List 7 ways, you will demonstrate to them that you are listening actively

Summary and Conclusions

Why is active listening important?
- How people speak is almost as important as what they say
- You can learn a lot from what people don't say
- Observing body language can reveal a lot
- You can make them feel more comfortable and build rapport
- Making them feel more relaxed will make them open up more

How to listen actively
- Prepare beforehand
- Set aside personal issues
- Acknowledge your emotions
- Exclude disruptions
- Forget your own opinions
- Set up the right environment
- Use non-visual cues
- Be involved
- Check your understanding and summarise

In conclusion

Fortunately the bosses at AGD Enterprises realised their mistake before it was too late. They took time to notice which people in the business they'd purchased could give them the information they needed.

They then took time to have some in-depth conversations that highlighted what had been going wrong in the business and they were able to minimise the losses as a result. They could only reflect on how much money they would have saved by listening more actively to what was going on during the purchase negotiations.

7.3 Keys to Coaching:
Why Questions are the Answer

John had been working hard to become managing director and when he made it at the age of just 35, everyone thought he had a great career ahead of him.

So his colleagues were shocked when just two years later, he quit the top position to do something entirely different.

Even his coach, who had been working so closely with him over these last few years, was stunned and disappointed.

As a coach, one of your aims is to help the client develop their own ideas and solutions. Therefore one of the most important skills of a good coach is being able to ask the right questions at the right time.

It follows that developing your questioning ability is one of the best ways of improving the results you get as a coach.

Why ask questions?
Here are some of the reasons why asking good questions is important.

- **Shows respect:** You are telling the client that you know they have the ideas and solutions within themselves. You're making clear that the relationship is not about you telling them what to do.

- **Makes them think**: People get easily caught up in their normal processes and asking questions is a way of breaking the pattern and making them consider new options.

- **Opens new possibilities**: The right questions will lead in directions that neither you nor the client would have considered without the question.

- **Sets direction**: Questions can keep a conversation on the right track and lead people in the direction you want them to go without being too directive.

- **Creates ownership**: Questions help the client to take responsibility both for coming up with the solutions and then for implementing them.

Different types of questions

There are several different types of question that you can use to get different results.

- **Closed**: A closed question is one where the answer options are limited – usually to a 'yes' or 'no' response. For example: "Did you enjoy that?"

- **Open**: An open question is one where the client can respond in any way they like. For example: "What do you think went well today?"

- **Funnelled**: A funnelled question is one which seeks to move from the general to the specific. For example: "Can you give me an example of what you mean?"

- **Probing**: A probing question seeks more detailed information about a situation. For example: "Tell me more about your experiences in that situation?"

- **Reflective**: A reflective question makes the client think more deeply about a situation. For example: "How do you think your team would feel about that?"

The key to asking questions
As well as knowing the right type of question to ask, a good coach knows how to ask questions.

The same question asked in different ways can seem aggressive and have the client on the defensive or it can open them up to consider new approaches.

Here are some of the ways to ask questions effectively:

- **Build rapport and relationships:** Take time to establish rapport and trust then be ready to judge the right moment to ask certain types of question.

- **Start with simple questions:** Don't rush into the difficult questions. Start with some easy and comfortable ones to prepare for more difficult ones later.

- **Use softening language:** Sometimes a difficult question can be asked more easily if couched in language such as "I'm wondering…" or "Wouldn't it be interesting if…"

- **Use empathetic body language:** Make sure your body language shows that you are with them and not working against them.

- **Don't apply blame:** Avoid accusing questions. Use questions that help people move forward.

Questions for different purposes

Here are some example questions that can be used in different situations.

- **Finding out the current situation**

    "How do you feel you are doing right now on scale of 1 – 10?"

    "What's going well right now – and what's going not so well?"

    "What is happening right now?"

- **Setting goals and objectives**

    "If you had already achieved what you want, what would it be like?"

    "If you had an unlimited amount of time and money, what would you do?"

    "Is this what you really want?"

- **Identifying obstacles**

    "What are you most afraid of?"

    "What is the best that can happen?"

    "What's preventing you from doing this?"

- **Creating opportunities**

    "What's one thing you could do to move forward now?"

    "Describe how it would be if everything was perfect?"

    "What would you do if you could start again?"

- **Solving problems**

    "What has worked for other people?"

    "Have you been in a situation like this before? What did you do"

    "What does your instinct tell you?"

- **Changing perspectives**

    "If someone else was in this situation, what would you say to them?"

    "What would you advise your best friend to do?"

    "What would a complete novice do?"

Case study: George the business owner

George had been running his own business for three years and was struggling financially as the business was not even breaking even.

George knew he had to take action and had to do it fast so he sat down with his business coach to find a way forward.

The coach could immediately see that George was doing badly because there were several steps he needed to take that he hadn't done.

- He wasn't out seeing enough prospective clients
- He wasn't charging enough for his time
- He was trying to do too much

The coach could have gone straight in and told George the problems but he knew that would not lead to him doing anything. Skilfully he worked through a range of questions with George to help him work out what was going wrong. Questions such as:

- What do you see others doing that you are not doing so well?
- What's stopping you from doing that?
- What benefits will you see when you do that?

Over several sessions, George identified where he needed to do things differently. He developed a plan to take some small steps in the areas that were holding him back. He started to get some support in areas where he was wasting too much time.

Quickly he got back on track and started attracting more clients, charging higher fees and making better use of his time.

Action step

1. Work out three questions of your own under each of the following headings.

- Finding out the current situation
- Setting goals and objectives
- Identifying obstacles
- Creating opportunities
- Solving problems
- Changing perspectives

2. Take three of the questions and work out five different ways of asking the same question.

Summary and Conclusions

Why ask questions?
- Shows respect
- Makes them think
- Opens new possibilities
- Sets direction
- Creates ownership

Different types of questions
- Closed
- Open
- Funnelled
- Probing
- Reflective

The key to asking questions
- Build rapport and relationships
- Start with simple questions
- Use softening language
- Use empathetic body language
- Don't apply blame

Conclusions

John's coach had helped him through all the steps necessary to get him into the top job.

John should have been grateful but after struggling to settle into the role, he realised there was one important question his coach had never asked.

In conversation with someone else, that most important question finally hit him: "Is that what you really want?"

His coach had done a great job of getting him to the goal he had stated. But the truth is John wanted to do something different with his life. He was just too busy to realise it and nobody had asked him.

7.4 Keys to Coaching:
Putting the Power of Many Brains to Work

The marketing team was shocked at the last quarter's sales figures that showed them losing their leading place in the market to their newest competitor.

They could have gone into a panic but instead decided to take a calmer view and got a group of the top salespeople together for a brainstorming session.

Why is brainstorming useful?

- **Provides a structured approach to find creative solutions:** While people often look for ways to come up with new ideas, it's not easy for most people just to sit down and become creative. The organised approach of brainstorming provides a framework where this is possible.

- **Allows different people to contribute:** While brainstorming can be done individually, it often works best as a combined effort where a range of different people make suggestions and evaluate ideas.

- **Generates a wide spread of ideas:** Whether done individually or in a group, brainstorming is a way of generating a lot of ideas quickly, many of which can be applied in other areas in addition to the specific task being considered.

- **Useful for team building:** As well as the ideas that are generated by team involvement in sessions, the process of working together has wider benefits in terms of co-operating and working together that build relationships over all issues

- **Encourages off-the-wall thinking:** Traditional business thinking is fairly conservative and the brainstorming approach encourages generation of a wider range of ideas that may often seem crazy at first but can turn out as extremely useful.

What is brainstorming?

Brainstorming is a technique for generating a large number of ideas for solutions to a problem. It is usually done in groups although individuals can follow the same principles to generate a lot of ideas.

The main principles of brainstorming are as follows:

- **Welcome any idea**: Ideas should not be evaluated at the time they are suggested. Anything can be suggested and evaluation should be done at a later stage in the process.

- **Encourage quantity**: At the first stage in the process, look for as many ideas as possible. Out of the large volume of ideas, you will later narrow the list down to the most appropriate. The more ideas you generate the better the chance of finding the right solution.

- **Look for unusual ideas**: Often looking at things from a completely different perspective can be a useful way of generating new solutions.

- **Build on suggestions**: Link ideas together and build on suggestions already made to create new combinations and improve on existing ideas.

The process of brainstorming

These are the steps to arrange a brainstorming session.

- **Define the problem:** Establish the precise problem or issue you want to resolve.

- **Choose participants:** Select the people you want to take part in the process based on the objectives you want to achieve. Groups of up to 10 people can work well and larger numbers can be split into sub-groups either to tackle the same problem or each can look at specific aspects of the issue.

- **Select a suitable venue:** Working in a relaxed and comfortable environment will assist the creativity process.

- **Brief the participants**: It's usually a good idea to let participants know in advance what the problem or issue is so that the creative process begins in advance.

- **Set the rules in advance:** make clear to everyone the way brainstorming works so that they are encouraged to come up with the widest possible range of ideas.

- **Record the ideas:** Have someone note the ideas as they are suggested. Tools such as postcards, flipcharts or Post-It notes are popular for brainstorming as they allow the suggestions to remain on display and be easily moved around.

- **Categorize ideas:** As the session develops move similar ideas into common categories to make it easier to combine and build on suggestions.

- **Review all the ideas:** Go through all the ideas to remove duplicates and look for final improvements.

- **Evaluate ideas:** Work through the ideas to identify the best solutions. There are a few steps to evaluation:

    o Clarify if suggestions are possible, using existing skills and resources.
    o If new resources are required, establish if that is possible
    o Score the proposed solutions using an appropriate scale such as A = High priority or 10 = Ideal Solution.
    o Rank the preferred solutions so that you end up with one solution or a number of prioritized solutions.
    o Identify steps and milestones for implementation of proposed solutions.

Individual brainstorming

The advantage of having a number of people brainstorming an idea – even if it is only two people – is that you have a range of minds working on the problem.

This is not always possibly or appropriate but the same principles can be used by an individual to generate a list of ideas.

Rather than working in a group, you set aside some time to generate a long list of ideas to tackle an issue and then follow a similar process of evaluation.

Individual brainstorming can use additional techniques to stimulate creativity such as free writing, word association or mind-mapping.

Case study: Susan's career change

Susan had been unhappy in her job for some time but was growing very frustrated with her lack of success in job interviews.

Talking the issue through with her life coach, she realised that she was looking in the wrong places and had to make a more significant change in her career choice.

At her coach's suggestion, she sat down one Sunday afternoon and used a range of different personal brainstorming techniques.

- Using free writing to go back over her past career experiences, she was able to identify what she really disliked about her job and what positive features she would look for in a new one.

- She then used idea generation to come up with a long list of her experiences from the past that supported that choice.

- Finally she brainstormed a list of potential employers to approach in this field and prioritized the 10 most likely to start with

A few months later, Susan loved her new role. That Sunday afternoon brainstorming changed her life for good.

Action step

- Think of an issue you or a client are currently facing and use the process of individual brainstorming to come up with a range of solutions.

Summary and Conclusions

Why is brainstorming useful?
- Provides a structured approach to find creative solutions
- Allows different people to contribute
- Generates a wide spread of ideas
- Useful for team building
- Encourages off-the-wall thinking

Principles of brainstorming
- Welcome any idea
- Encourage quantity
- Look for unusual ideas
- Build on suggestions

The process of brainstorming
- Define the problem
- Choose participants
- Select a suitable venue
- Brief the participants
- Set the rules in advance
- Record the ideas
- Categorize ideas
- Review all the ideas
- Evaluate ideas

Conclusions

In the brainstorming session with the sales team, they were able to identify three quick changes they could make to the product without increasing the cost. Next quarter, sales were back to normal and they were back in a market-leading position.

7.5 Keys to Coaching:
How to Get Action When Nothing Else Works

Joe set up his own consulting business more than a year ago and he's been busy setting up his website, his marketing plans and his internal systems – but he doesn't have any clients.

When he sat down with his coach, he said it was hard to explain why things were going so badly. He'd been busy all year and just needed a bit more time to get things sorted out.

Why is taking action important?

- **People get distracted:** Even when people have plans in place, they find it easy to find something 'more important' to do. Many need a discipline to make them do what's most important.

- **Action leads to momentum:** Often taking that first step is all that's needed to create a regular habit and get someone moving towards their goal.

- **Procrastination is rife:** Many people suffer from that problem of putting off until a later date something they should do today. This becomes a habit that prevents them achieving their goals.

- **We avoid things we don't like:** Most people delay doing things they don't enjoy – whether it's calling prospects or preparing the tax return. This becomes a big underlying problem for the business, as important tasks never get done.

How to we encourage action?
One of the coach's most important tasks is to encourage clients to get

things done. There are several techniques that can be used to help this, including:

- **Detailed action plan:** Often the big problem is not knowing what to do next. A step-by-step action plan breaks down the tasks so that everyone knows exactly what to do.

- **Public commitment:** Making a public commitment to do something provides a strong motivation to make something happen. Sometimes the commitment could be just to one person, for others it could be making a general announcement that something is going to happen on a specific date. The more public the commitment, the greater the motivation.

- **Reward or punishment:** You can encourage someone to take action by making them commit to a reward for doing it or punishment for not doing it. For example, if you complete this by Friday, go out for a nice dinner that night. If you don't finish it, cancel your Saturday night out.

- **Accountability partner:** Get someone to commit to action by arranging a daily call with an accountability partner to explain what they did the day before and what they are going to do that day.

- **Daily measurement:** Keeping a daily journal or keeping daily statistics can encourage people to do something every day. They see the progress they are making and this encourages more action.

Case study: The customer services team

The customer services team was facing a huge backlog of customer complaints which was having a negative effect on the team and making service even worse.

The team got together and worked out a strategy for how they were going to improve the situation. They needed to find a solution that got fast results and kept everyone motivated.

They introduced a number of techniques.

- Worked out a step by step action plan for tackling it

- Made a public commitment to clear the backlog by a specific date

- Tracked the daily reduction in the backlog to maintain motivation

- Planned a big social event to happen when the backlog was cleared

As a result of this process, they cleared the backlog two weeks before the published date and enjoyed a great party to celebrate.

Action step

- Think of an issue you or a client are currently facing and work out a series of specific steps to encourage fast action.

Summary and Conclusions

Why is taking action important?
- People get distracted
- Action leads to momentum
- Procrastination is rife
- We avoid things we don't like

How to we encourage action?
- Detailed action plan
- Public commitment
- Reward or punishment
- Accountability partner
- Daily measurement

Conclusions

Joe's coach pointed out to him that he was busy but he was busy doing the wrong things.

He wasn't taking enough action on the things that were important. For example, he was spending too much time on his website and not enough time contacting prospective clients.

Deep down, Joe knew this already. He hated the idea of selling and just didn't want to take the steps needed.

Together the agreed a strategy of 'one thing a day' and gradually contacting prospects became a comfortable part of his daily routine. Now he's too busy working with clients to keep that website looking good.

7.6 Keys to Coaching:
How to Clear Immovable Obstacles on the Road to Success

David had some great ideas about how to increase his sales but the marketing manager didn't like his ideas and wouldn't give him a budget.

Even though he was one of the top sales people, David had no marketing budget of his own and the marketing team wouldn't fund his ideas.

He was very frustrated as he was totally confident they would work but without funding he couldn't see a way forward.

Why are overcoming obstacles important?

- **Obstacles always occur:** Even the best plans hit unexpected situations or people who are not willing to co-operate. If we're not prepared to find a way round these problems, we won't achieve our objectives.

- **Obstacles are a sign of progress:** You only start to hit obstacles when you are moving forward and the more progress you make the more obstacles you will hit. That's why it's vital to have strategies for clearing them.

- **Obstacles will multiply:** If you give in to problems, this will become a habit. At first the problems will be large obstacles but over time small hassles will stop you taking any action.

- **Obstacles can be useful:** Often having to find a solution to a problem has many side benefits – both in terms of new processes discovered and in team building.

How to overcome obstacles

The best strategy will obviously depend on the exact obstacle and the person or people involved. But there are several strategies you can call on to move forward:

- **More people / resources:** In some cases, you may just need to put more time, money or people onto a problem to remove the obstacle.

- **Change the people:** When circumstances change, consider whether the people involved have the right skills and mindset. Sometimes a different situation benefits from having new people involved.

- **Creative solutions:** Discover other ways to solve the problem if your preferred approach doesn't work. This can sometimes lead to even better solutions.

- **Re-evaluate the situation:** Stop to think about whether the outcome you are going for is the right one or whether it can be adapted to take account of the new situation you are in.

- **Plan ahead for problems:** Before starting on a project, consider all the likely outcomes and all the things that could go wrong. Plan strategies in advance to avoid them or to deal with them.

Case study: Anna's restaurant

Anna had been running the restaurant for three months and was excited about the way the number of customers was increasing.

The only problem was that she worried about how slow the service was.

It seemed the chef was a bit of a perfectionist and was doing everything slowly to make sure it was just right.

She considered the option of encouraging him to change his ways but people really loved the food. She also considered a new chef but this would involve a lot of risk.

When she sat down with her coach to work out a way round the problem, she realised that it could be more of an opportunity.

She had a great chef and people liked his food so rather than trying to get him to change, she changed the restaurant to work with his style.

She put the emphasis on his perfectionism and on the quality of the food and ended up increasing the prices.

Over time, she discovered that even more people loved that approach and they were busier than ever. But the key is people came knowing they would be getting great food and nobody complained about having to wait for that.

What seemed like an obstacle turned into a very profitable opportunity.

Action step

- Consider a problem that you – or a client – are currently facing that is stopping you from making progress. Brainstorm a number of ways of responding to the challenge so that you either make progress or review the plan.

Summary and Conclusions

Why are overcoming obstacles important?
- Obstacles always occur
- Obstacles are a sign of progress
- Obstacles will multiply
- Obstacles can be useful

How to overcome obstacles
- More people / resources
- Change the people
- Creative solutions
- Re-evaluate the situation
- Plan ahead for problems

Conclusions

When Dave thought more about it, he realised that his idea did not require much money.

He therefore set about implementing it without asking for a budget and his hunch proved right.

A few weeks later, the marketing team had sent someone to learn about what he was doing so that they could apply it across the company.

7.7 Keys to Coaching:
Making Feedback the Key to Getting Results

Sally had been working as his personal assistant for nearly five months and Bob couldn't understand why she kept making the same mistakes.

She was doing most of the job really well but there were a few small but important tasks that she wasn't doing the way he wanted.

He kept telling her how to do it differently and he was getting frustrated that she wasn't paying any attention.

Why is feedback important?

- **External perspective:** People don't know how they are doing until someone tells them. They often work on the basis that if nobody complains everything is fine. It's only through proper feedback that can people can get a perspective of what is working well and what needs to change.

- **Motivational:** When people are told what they do well, they are motivated to keep doing that and to make changes to things that are not going well.

- **Self-correction:** Feedback allows people to change their own behaviour and to experiment with different ways of doing things. This is only possible when someone tells them what is going well and what needs to be different.

- **Continual improvement:** Feedback is not just about when things are going well. It should be an ongoing learning process that allows people to focus on how results can be improved.

Keys to feedback

- **Fast:** Feedback should be as soon as possible after an event happens. If there is no opportunity for detailed feedback at that point, provide some quick feedback and agree to follow it up as soon as possible in more detail.

- **Specific:** make references to specific instances and actions. Generalisations are not helpful as people can't relate to them and take action on them.

- **Positive focus:** Feedback should put the emphasis on what is going well. A good feedback session will begin and end with encouraging comments about what the person has done well.

- **Concentrate of action not the person:** It should be clear that feedback is about what the person does, not who they are. You are teaching them to do something differently – not to change them as a person.

- **Future focus:** Feedback should concentrate on what they can do differently next time not on what went wrong last time.

- **Make suggestions:** In giving feedback, you should use the language of suggestion rather than the language of blame. You are helping them to identify new options not to criticise them for options they have chosen previously.

- **Avoid debate:** Though it may be appropriate to allow the person to comment on feedback, debate about why they did it is not helpful.

The client should be invited to take the feedback on board rather than argue about whether it is valid or make excuses for why something happened.

Checking

An important part of feedback is checking in with the other person.

This can apply in several ways:

- **Checking how they felt it went:** Before giving external feedback, it can be useful to ask the client how they feel about something. Let them identify areas where they think improvement is needed or where it went well for them.

- **Checking they understand the feedback:** after giving feedback ask to make sure they are clear about what it means. Don't ask if they agree with it but check to make sure they are focusing on what's important.

- **Checking what they plan to do next time:** Find out what action the person plans to take next time they are in the same situation. This is partly a check of understanding and partly a commitment by them.

- **Checking they are happy with the process:** Make sure they are comfortable with how the coaching or feedback process is working. This is not about whether they like the feedback but about whether it is working for them.

- **Checking if there is anything else:** Make sure the feedback has covered everything the client wants to cover. Ask if there is anything else they want to cover.

How to give feedback

The main steps involved in giving feedback are as follows:

- Start with an overall positive comment and address some specific things that went well

- Point out some specific aspects that could be done differently next time to get an even better result

- Finish with an encouraging and upbeat motivational point

In some cases, it's appropriate to add a checking step:

- Ask them to confirm what they will do differently next time

Case study: Alan the sales manager

Alan had been one of the top sales consultants last year and was now completing his first six months as area manager.

Mike, his sales director, had left him to get on with it and things were not going as well as either of them hoped.

Mike's initial reaction was to blame himself for promoting Alan realising that good sales people often make poor managers. However something told him Alan was different. So he sat down with Alan and pointed out:

- He was one of their top salespeople and that his relationships with his clients were vital to the success of the business.

- As a manager now his priority was to develop his team of salespeople to be as successful as he was.

- He needed to put the same effort into training and developing his own people as he had previously made with his clients.

- He was very popular with the team and was in a great position to do this.

When they had this conversation, Alan was initially shocked and distressed. He could see that things weren't going too well and he was desperate to get back to his old role.

But from the feedback, he realised how he needed to tackle the job differently and he immediately began changing the way he worked. By the year-end, his team was top in the region.

Action step

- Consider an issue where you need to give feedback to a client and decide how to structure it best for maximum impact.

Summary and Conclusions

Why is feedback important?
- External perspective
- Motivational
- Self-correction
- Continual improvement

Keys to feedback
- Fast
- Specific
- Positive focus
- Concentrate of action not the person
- Future focus
- Make suggestions
- Avoid debate

Checking
- Checking how they felt it went
- Checking they understand the feedback
- Checking what they plan to do next time
- Checking they are happy with the process
- Checking if there is anything else

Conclusions

Bob talked it over with his business coach. "Why won't she do it the way I want?" he asked. "I keep telling her what she needs to do differently."

"Well," said his coach. "You say she's doing most of the job well. Have you tried telling her what's she's doing right."

Bob was stunned for a moment. He'd never thought of that. He sort of assumed she realised that he was happy – he'd tell her if there was a problem.

So over the next few days, he focused his comments on what she was doing well. And gradually he began to add in a few suggestions on what she could do even better.

The only problem is she's now doing the job so well, he's having to think about promoting her into a new role!

8. The Process of Coaching

Two vital factors in a coaching relationship are deciding how best to deliver the coaching and how often to do it.

There are a number of ways in which you can provide coaching and the best will depend on the required outcome and the budget available. Several different methods can be used together.

- **Face-to-face coaching:** Personal coaching sessions are the high end of the offer as they are naturally more time-consuming and expensive. A monthly meeting could be supplemented by regular telephone and email access.

- **Telephone coaching:** Telephone coaching works well on its own or alongside another type of coaching. It has some of the personal advantages of meetings with the time benefits of being by telephone. Calls can either be scheduled at specific times or arranged to deal with issues that arise.

- **Email coaching:** Email is particularly valuable if there are documents to review or if it is one simple question that requires a quick answer. It has the advantage that both parties can respond when it is convenient to them – they don't need to both be free at the same time.

- **Team coaching:** Some coaching is best done in groups, particularly if it involves team issues or culture change. Working with a team can involve always being as a team or it can include individual sessions with some or all of the members.

How often

The key to how often coaching should occur depends on the budget and on the desired outcome.

It also depends on whether a mix of different types of coaching is being used.

Personal meetings may be once or twice a month but telephone and email access may be more frequent.

Many coaches would operate with a fixed program of a set number of meetings then have some agreement about access in-between times.

When good coaching involves clear structures and action plans, the client can make significant progress outside of the meeting environment.

9. Developing a Coaching Mission Statement

As a coach, you will be using many tools to develop and shape your practice. One of the most important tools you can use to define your business at the onset is the coaching mission statement. This brief statement will help you understand your business and develop a framework for attracting and working with clients.

Your coaching mission statement should answer three questions:

- What are the needs or problems I solve through my coaching practice? (Essentially, what is the purpose of my business?)
- What am I doing to solve those needs or problems?
- What are the principles or beliefs that guide my work?

The exercise of working through these questions and distilling the answers into a concise, targeted mission statement can seem a bit overwhelming. Indeed, it does take some time to develop a coaching mission statement, but it doesn't necessarily have to be difficult. Let's look at an example:

Joe is starting a career coaching practice. As he sits down to write his mission statement, he addresses the three questions:

- *What needs or problems do I solve?* I help mid-career professionals redirect and discover new career choices when they lose their jobs or become unsatisfied with their work.
- *What am I doing to solve those needs or problems?* I provide clients with the resources, tools, encouragement, and motivation to explore their needs, aspirations, and career goals. Through self-assessment, I help

clients discover new career paths, and help them develop the strategies necessary to embark on the path of achieving their career goals.
- *What are the principles or beliefs that guide my work?* Every individual has the right to find meaningful, inspiring, rewarding work. Additionally, every person has the capacity to utilize self-assessment and personal exploration to find the work that he or she is meant to perform.

He can then use this information to craft his coaching mission statement. Distilling these points into a brief statement is no easy task, but through careful writing and rewriting, it can be accomplished. Joe's coaching mission statement might look like this:

"To help mid-career professionals discover and embark on new career paths through self assessment, empowering them to exercise their right and capacity to enjoy fulfilling work."

The mission statement might also use bullet points to address each of the three questions:

- *Purpose: To help mid-career professionals discover and embark upon new career paths.*
- *Method: Empowering professionals to engage in self-assessment and personal awareness.*
- *Core Beliefs: Every individual has the right and capacity to engage in fulfilling, meaningful work.*

How would you answer the three questions about your business? Take the time to brainstorm and develop targeted answers as they relate to your coaching practice. Then identify the key points and use them to craft a powerful mission statement. This will help you, your clients and the public understand what your business is about, and how it can be a benefit to others.

A

Accountability, 12, 70, 73
ACHIEVE, 33, 36, 37, 39, 41, 43, 44
Action, 5, 27, 36, 43, 51, 59, 67, 69, 72, 73, 77, 84
active listening, 47, 50, 51, 52
Awareness, 4, 22, 25

B

body language, 47, 52, 55, 60
brainstorming, 62, 63, 64, 65, 66, 67, 68
Business coaching, 4, 16
businesses, 3, 4, 7, 9, 10, 11, 13

C

career, 6, 9, 10, 11, 32, 44, 53, 66, 89, 90
Case study, 42, 50, 58, 66, 71, 76, 83
Challenge, 4, 13, 23, 25
Character, 5, 28
Clarity, 4, 5, 12, 22, 25, 26
clients, 3, 6, 11, 16, 18, 19, 23, 32, 38, 40, 42, 58, 69, 73, 83, 89, 90
closed question, 54
COACH model, 5, 26
coaching session, 26
commitment, 30, 44, 70, 71, 73, 81
Compassion, 4, 24, 25
Confidence, 4, 12, 22, 25
consulting, 19, 69
Contacts, 12
counselling, 4, 20
Creativity, 4, 23, 25, 33, 44
Curiosity, 4, 22, 25

D

Detachment, 4, 24, 25

E

Ecological, 36, 44
emotions, 20, 48, 52
Empathy, 4, 23, 25
encouragement, 30, 89
entrepreneurs, 10, 17
Evaluating, 25
Exciting, 35, 44
Executive coaching, 4, 17

F

feedback, 4, 5, 15, 79, 80, 81, 82, 83, 84, 85
funnelled question, 54

G

goal, 8, 26, 28, 29, 30, 31, 32, 33, 34, 35, 36, 37, 38, 39, 40, 41, 43, 44, 45, 61, 69

I

Integrity, 4, 23, 25
intentions, 38
Internal coaching, 4, 17

J

John F Kennedy, 29
judging, 34

L

Life coaching, 4, 18
Listening, 15

M

management, 9, 17, 18, 46
managers, 17, 83
measurement, 30, 44, 70, 73
mentor, 21
milestones, 30, 40, 65
millionaire, 34
mission statement, 5, 89, 90
Motivation, 12

O

Obstacles, 74, 78
open question, 54
Options, 5, 27
organisation, 6, 9, 11, 12, 13, 17, 18
Organisations, 9
outcomes, 4, 14, 37, 38, 44, 75

P

Patience, 4, 23, 25
performance, 2, 3, 11, 12, 16, 38, 44
performance coaches, 16
Personal coaching, 87
Personality, 4, 24, 25
principles, 63, 65, 89, 90
probing question, 54
psychology, 16

Q

questions, 5, 13, 18, 23, 26, 27, 49, 53, 54, 55, 56, 58, 59, 60, 89, 90, 93

R

rapport, 47, 52, 55, 60
reflective question, 54
relationship, 8, 14, 16, 18, 23, 24, 26, 36, 53, 87
resources, 12, 28, 37, 40, 43, 45, 65, 75, 78, 89, 93

S

strategies, 1, 6, 8, 41, 74, 75, 89

success, 5, 6, 7, 14, 19, 39, 42, 45, 46, 66, 83

T

Team building, 12
techniques, 1, 2, 6, 8, 9, 48, 65, 66, 70, 71
Telephone coaching, 87
Therapy, 4, 20
Tony Robbins, 8
Training, 2, 3, 4, 19, 93

U

unconscious mind, 37

V

Verifiable, 35, 44

W

Wikipedia, 8

You are invited to visit www.free-nlp.co.uk to discover a range of resources including CDs, DVDs and books on related subjects.

Training Excellence offers the highest standard in training, which includes:

NLP Level 1
NLP Practitioner
NLP Master Practitioner
Coaching Practitioner
Corporate Coaching
Hypnosis Practitioner
Hypnosis Master Practitioner
Public Speaking

We would like to thank you for purchasing this book and if you have any questions or would like to share your experiences of using NLP Language Patterns with us please email john@free-nlp.co.uk

Also download our free iPhone app, NLP Dictionary.

Kind regards

John